The G
Authority

Authority in the Church III

An Agreed Statement by the
Anglican – Roman Catholic International Commission
A R C I C

Published for the Anglican Consultative Council
and the Pontifical Council for Promoting Christian Unity

  CTS

 CHURCH

Catholic Truth Society
Publishers to the
Holy See, London

Anglican Book Centre
Toronto, Canada

Church Publishing
Incorporated
New York

1999
Anglican Book Centre
600 Jarvis Street
Toronto, Ontario
Canada M4Y 2J6

1999
Catholic Truth Society
40–46 Harleyford Road
London, SE11 5AY

1999
Church Publishing
Incorporated
445 Fifth Avenue
New York, NY 10016

Canadian Cataloguing in Publication

Anglican/Roman Catholic International Commission
  The gift of authority: authority in the church III

Co-published by the Catholic Truth Society and Church Publishing.
ISBN 1-55126-246-0

1. Church — Authority — Congresses. 2. Papacy — Congresses. 3. Pope — Infallibility — Congresses. 4. Catholic Church — Relations — Anglican Communion — Congresses. 5. Anglican Communion — Relations — Catholic Church — Congresses. I. Catholic Truth Society of Canada. II. Title.

BT91.A534 1999   262'.8   C99-930593-X

ISBN 1-55126-246-0 (ABC)
ISBN 1 86082 058 1 (CTS)
ISBN 0-89869-325-X (CPI)

CONTENTS

PREFACE

By the Co-Chairmen

An earnest search for full visible unity between the Anglican Communion and the Roman Catholic Church was initiated over thirty years ago by the historic meeting in Rome of Archbishop Michael Ramsey and Pope Paul VI. The Commission set up to prepare for the dialogue recognised, in its 1968 *Malta Report*, that one of the "urgent and important tasks" would be to examine the question of authority. In a sense, this question is at the heart of our sad divisions.

When *The Final Report* of ARCIC (Anglican-Roman Catholic International Commission) was published in 1981, half of it was devoted to the dialogue about authority in the Church, with two agreed statements and an elucidation. This was important groundwork, preparing the way for further convergence. The official responses, by the 1988 Lambeth Conference of the Anglican Communion and by the Catholic Church in 1991, encouraged the Commission to carry forward the "remarkable progress" that had been made. Accordingly ARCIC now offers this further agreed statement, *The Gift of Authority*.

A scriptural image is the key to this statement. In chapter one of his second letter to the Corinthians, Paul writes of God's "Yes" to humanity and our answering "Amen" to God, both given in Jesus Christ (cf. 2 Cor 1.19–20). God's gift of authority to his Church is at the service of God's "Yes" to his people and their "Amen."

The reader is invited to follow the path that led the Commission to its conclusions. They are the fruit of five years of dialogue, of patient listening, study, and prayer together. The statement will, we hope, prompt further theological reflection; its conclusions present a challenge to our two Churches, not least in regard to the crucial issue of universal primacy. Authority is about how the Church teaches, acts and reaches doctrinal decisions in faithfulness to the Gospel, so real agreement about authority cannot be theoretical. If this statement is to contribute to the reconciliation of the Anglican Communion and the Catholic Church and is accepted, it will require a response in life and in deed.

Much has happened over these years to deepen our awareness of each other as brothers and sisters in Christ. Yet our journey towards full, visible unity is proving longer than some expected and many hoped. We have encountered serious obstacles that make progress difficult. At such a stage, the persevering, painstaking work of dialogue is all the more vital. The present Archbishop of Canterbury, Dr George Carey, and Pope John Paul II stated very frankly the need for this work on authority when they met in 1996: "Without agreement in this area we shall not reach the full, visible unity to which we are both committed."

We pray that God will enable the Commission's work to contribute to the end we all desire, the healing of our divisions so that together we may say a united "'Amen' to the glory of God" (2 Cor 1.20).

+Cormac Murphy-O'Connor
+Mark Santer

Palazzola
Feast of St Gregory the Great
ember 1998

THE STATUS OF THE DOCUMENT

The Document published here is the work of the Anglican–Roman Catholic International Commission (ARCIC). It is a joint statment of the Commission. The authorities who appointed the Commission have allowed the statement to be published so that it may be widely discussed. It is not an authoritative declaration by the Roman Catholic Church or by the Anglican Communion, who will evaluate the document in order to take a position on it in due time.

Citations from Scripture are from the New Revised Standard Version.

INTRODUCTION

1. The dialogue between Anglicans and Roman Catholics has shown significant signs of progress on the question of authority in the Church. This progress can already be seen in the convergence in understanding of authority achieved by previous ARCIC statements, notably:

- acknowledgement that the Spirit of the Risen Lord maintains the people of God in obedience to the Father's will. By this action of the Holy Spirit, the authority of the Lord is active in the Church (cf. *The Final Report, Authority in the Church I*, 3);
- a recognition that because of their baptism and their participation in the *sensus fidelium*, the laity play an integral part in decision making in the Church (cf. *Authority in the Church: Elucidation*, 4);
- the complementarity of primacy and conciliarity as elements of *episcope* within the Church (cf. *Authority in the Church I*, 22);
- the need for a universal primacy exercised by the Bishop of Rome as a sign and safeguard of unity within a reunited Church (cf. *Authority in the Church II*, 9);
- the need for the universal primate to exercise his ministry in collegial association with the other bishops (cf. *Authority in the Church II*, 19);
- an understanding of universal primacy and conciliarity which complements and does not supplant the exercise of *episcope* in local churches (cf. *Authority in the Church I*, 21-23; *Authority in the Church II*, 19).

2. This convergence has been officially noted by the authorities of the Anglican Communion and the Roman Catholic Church. The Lambeth Conference, meeting in 1988, not only saw the ARCIC

agreements on eucharistic doctrine and on ministry and ordination as consonant in substance with the faith of Anglicans (*Resolution 8:1*) but affirmed that the agreed statements on authority in the church provided a basis for further dialogue (*Resolution 8:3*). Similarly, the Holy See, in its official response of 1991, recognising areas of agreement on questions of very great importance for the faith of the Roman Catholic Church, such as the Eucharist and the Church's ministry, noted the signs of convergence between our two communions on the question of authority in the Church, indicating that this opened the way to further progress.

3. However, the authorities of our two communions have asked for further exploration of areas where, although there has been convergence, they believe that a necessary consensus has not yet been achieved. These areas include:

- the relationship between Scripture, Tradition and the exercise of teaching authority;
- collegiality, conciliarity, and the role of laity in decision making;
- the Petrine ministry of universal primacy in relation to Scripture and Tradition.

Even though progress has been made, some serious difficulties have emerged on the way to unity. Issues concerning authority have been raised acutely for each of our communions. For example, debates and decisions about the ordination of women have led to questions about the sources and structures of authority and how they function for Anglicans and Roman Catholics.

4. In both communions the exploration of how authority should be exercised at different levels has been open to the perspectives of other churches on these issues. For example, *The Virginia Report* of the Inter-Anglican Theological and Doctrinal Commission (prepared for the Lambeth Conference of 1998) declares:

"The long history of ecumenical involvement, both locally and internationally, has shown us that Anglican discernment and decision making must take account of the insights into truth and the Spirit-led wisdom of our ecumenical partners. Moreover, any decisions we take must be offered for the discernment of the universal Church" (*The Virginia Report*, 6.37).

Pope John Paul II also, in his Encyclical Letter *Ut Unum Sint*, invited leaders and theologians of other churches to engage with him in a fraternal dialogue on how the particular ministry of unity of the Bishop of Rome might be exercised in a new situation (cf. *Ut Unum Sint*, 95–96).

5. There is an extensive debate about the nature and exercise of authority both in the churches and in wider society. Anglicans and Roman Catholics want to witness, both to the churches and to the world, that authority rightly exercised is a gift of God to bring reconciliation and peace to humankind. The exercise of authority can be oppressive and destructive. It may, indeed, often be so in human societies and even in churches when they uncritically adopt certain patterns of authority. The exercise of authority in the ministry of Jesus shows a different way. It is in conformity with the mind and example of Christ that the Church is called to exercise authority (cf. Lk 22.24–27; Jn 13.14–15; Phil 2.1–11). For the exercise of this authority the Church is endowed by the Holy Spirit with a variety of gifts and ministries (cf. 1 Cor 12.4–11; Eph 4.11–12).

6. From the beginning of its work, ARCIC has considered questions of Church teaching or practice in the context of our real but imperfect communion in Christ and the visible unity to which we are called. The Commission has always sought to get behind opposed and entrenched positions to discover and develop our com-

mon inheritance. Building on the previous work of ARCIC, the Commission offers a further statement on how the gift of authority, rightly exercised, enables the Church to continue in obedience to the Holy Spirit, who keeps it faithful in the service of the Gospel for the salvation of the world. We wish further to clarify how the exercise and acceptance of authority in the Church is inseparable from the response of believers to the Gospel, how it is related to the dynamic interaction of Scripture and Tradition, and how it is expressed and experienced in the communion of the churches and the collegiality of their bishops. In the light of these insights we have come to a deepened understanding of a universal primacy which serves the unity of all the local churches.

II. AUTHORITY IN THE CHURCH

Jesus Christ: God's "Yes" to Us and our "Amen" to God

7. God is the author of life. By his Word and Spirit, in perfect freedom, God calls life into being. In spite of human sin, God in perfect faithfulness remains the author of the hope of new life for all. In Jesus Christ's work of redemption God renews his promise to his creation, for "God's purpose is to bring all people into communion with himself within a transformed creation" (ARCIC, *Church as Communion*, 16). The Spirit of God continues to work in creation and redemption to bring this purpose of reconciliation and unity to completion. The root of all true authority is thus the activity of the triune God, who authors life in all its fullness.

8. The authority of Jesus Christ is that of the "faithful witness," the "Amen" (cf. Rev 1.5; 3.14) in whom all the promises of God find their "Yes." When Paul had to defend the authority of his teaching he did so by pointing to the trustworthy authority of God: "As surely as God is faithful, our word to you has not been Yes and No. For the Son of God, Jesus Christ, whom we preached among you... was not Yes and No; but in him it is always Yes. For all the promises of God find their Yes in him. That is why we utter the Amen through him, to the glory of God" (2 Cor 1.18–20). Paul speaks of the "Yes" of God to us and the "Amen" of the Church to God. In Jesus Christ, Son of God and born of a woman, the "Yes" of God to humanity and the "Amen" of humanity to God become a concrete human reality. This theme of God's "Yes" and humanity's "Amen" in Jesus Christ is the key to the exposition of authority in this statement.

9. In the life and ministry of Jesus, who came to do his Father's will (cf. Heb 10.5–10) even unto death (cf. Phil 2.8; Jn 10.18), God pro-

vided the perfect human "Amen" to his purpose of reconciliation. In his life, Jesus expressed his total dedication to the Father (cf. Jn 5.19). The way Jesus exercised authority in his earthly ministry was perceived by his contemporaries as something new. It was recognised in his powerful teaching and in his healing and liberating word (cf. Mt 7.28–29; Mk 1.22, 27). Most of all, his authority was demonstrated by his self-giving service in sacrificial love (cf. Mk 10.45). Jesus spoke and acted with authority because of his perfect communion with the Father. His authority came from the Father (cf. Mt 11.27; Jn 14.10–12). It is to the Risen Lord that all authority is given in heaven and on earth (cf. Mt 28.18). Jesus Christ now lives and reigns with the Father, in the unity of the Holy Spirit; he is the Head of his Body, the Church, and Lord of all Creation (cf. Eph 1.18–23).

10. The life-giving obedience of Jesus Christ calls forth through the Spirit our "Amen" to God the Father. In this "Amen" through Christ we glorify God, who gives the Spirit in our hearts as a pledge of his faithfulness (cf. 2 Cor 1.20–22). We are called in Christ to witness to God's purpose (cf. Lk 24.46–49), a witness that may for us too include obedience to the point of death. In Christ obedience is not a burden (cf. 1 Jn 5.3). It springs from the liberation given by the Spirit of God. The divine "Yes" and our "Amen" are clearly seen in baptism, when in the company of the faithful we say "Amen" to God's work in Christ. By the Spirit, our "Amen" as believers is incorporated in the "Amen" of Christ, through whom, with whom, and in whom we worship the Father.

The Believer's "Amen" in the "Amen" of the Local Church

11. The Gospel comes to people in a variety of ways: the witness and life of a parent or other Christian, the reading of the Scriptures, participation in the liturgy, or some other spiritual experience. Acceptance of the Gospel is also enacted in many ways: in being baptised, in renewal of commitment, in a decision to remain faithful, or

in acts of self-giving to those in need. In these actions the person says, "Indeed, Jesus Christ is *my* God: he is *for me* salvation, the source of hope, the true face of the living God."

12. When a believer says "Amen" to Christ individually, a further dimension is always involved: an "Amen" to the faith of the Christian community. The person who receives baptism must come to know the full implication of participating in divine life within the Body of Christ. The believer's "Amen" to Christ becomes yet more complete as that person receives all that the Church, in faithfulness to the Word of God, affirms to be the authentic content of divine revelation. In that way, the "Amen" said to what Christ is *for each believer* is incorporated within the "Amen" the Church says to what Christ is *for his Body*. Growing into this faith may be for some an experience of questioning and struggle. For all it is one in which the integrity of the believer's conscience has a vital part to play. The believer's "Amen" to Christ is so fundamental that individual Christians throughout their life are called to say "Amen" to all that the whole company of Christians receives and teaches as the authentic meaning of the Gospel and the way to follow Christ.

13. Believers follow Christ in communion with other Christians in their local church (cf. *Authority in the Church I*, 8, where it is explained that 'the unity of local communities under one bishop constitutes what is commonly meant in our two communions by 'a local church''). In the local church they share Christian life, together finding guidance for the formation of their conscience and strength to face their difficulties. They are sustained by the means of grace which God provides for his people: the Holy Scriptures, expounded in preaching, catechesis and creeds; the sacraments; the service of the ordained ministry; the life of prayer and common worship; the witness of holy persons. The believer is incorporated into an "Amen" of faith, older, deeper, broader, richer than the individual's "Amen" to the Gospel. So the relation between the faith of the individual and the faith of the Church is more complex than may sometimes

appear. Every baptised person shares the rich experience of the Church which, even when it struggles with contemporary questions, continues to proclaim what Christ is *for his Body*. Each believer, by the grace of the Spirit, together with all believers of all times and all places, inherits this faith of the Church in the communion of saints. Believers then live out a twofold "Amen" within the continuity of worship, teaching and practice of their local church. This local church is a eucharistic community. At the centre of its life is the celebration of the Holy Eucharist in which all believers hear and receive God's "Yes" in Christ to them. In the Great Thanksgiving, when the memorial of God's gift in the saving work of Christ crucified and risen is celebrated, the community is at one with all Christians of all the churches who, since the beginning and until the end, pronounce humanity's "Amen" to God — the "Amen" which the Apocalypse affirms is at the heart of the great liturgy of heaven (cf. Rev 5.14; 7.12).

Tradition and Apostolicity: The Local Church's "Amen" in the Communion of the Churches

14. The "Yes" of God commands and invites the "Amen" of believers. The revealed Word, to which the apostolic community originally bore witness, is received and communicated through the life of the whole Christian community. Tradition (*paradosis*) refers to this process.[1] The

---

[1] In accord with ecumenical usage, the capitalised word *Tradition* here refers to "the Gospel itself, transmitted from generation to generation in and by the Church," while the uncapitalised word *tradition* refers to "the traditionary process," the handing-on of the revealed truth (The Fourth World Conference on Faith and Order, Montreal 1963, Section II, para. 39). The plural *traditions* refers to the peculiar features of liturgy, theology, canonical and ecclesial life in the various cultures and faith communities. These uses, however, often cannot be sharply distinguished. When "tradition" is capitalised at the beginning of a sentence, context must determine sense. The phrase *apostolic Tradition* refers to the content of what has been transmitted from apostolic times and continues to be the foundation of Christian life and theology.

Gospel of Christ crucified and risen is continually handed on and received (cf. 1 Cor 15.3) in the Christian churches. This tradition, or handing on, of the Gospel is the work of the Spirit, especially through the ministry of Word and Sacrament and in the common life of the people of God. Tradition is a dynamic process, communicating to each generation what was delivered once for all to the apostolic community. Tradition is far more than the transmission of true propositions concerning salvation. A minimalist understanding of Tradition that would limit it to a storehouse of doctrine and ecclesial decisions is insufficient. The Church receives, and must hand on, all those elements that are constitutive of ecclesial communion: baptism, confession of the apostolic faith, celebration of the Eucharist, leadership by an apostolic ministry (cf. *Church as Communion*, 15, 43). In the economy (*oikonomia*) of God's love for humanity, the Word who became flesh and dwelt among us is at the centre of what was transmitted from the beginning and what will be transmitted until the end.

15. Tradition is a channel of the love of God, making it accessible in the Church and in the world today. Through it, from one generation to another, and from one place to another, humanity shares communion in the Holy Trinity. By the process of tradition, the Church ministers the grace of the Lord Jesus Christ and the *koinonia* of the Holy Spirit (cf. 2 Cor 13.14). Therefore Tradition is integral to the economy of grace, love and communion. For those whose ears have not heard and eyes have not seen, the moment of receiving the saving Gospel is an experience of enlightenment, forgiveness, healing, liberation. Those who participate in the communion of the Gospel cannot refrain from transmitting it to others, even if this means martyrdom. Tradition is both a treasure to be received by the people of God and a gift to be shared with all humanity.

16. Apostolic Tradition is a gift of God which must be constantly received anew. By means of it, the Holy Spirit forms, maintains and sustains the communion of the local churches from one generation to the next. The handing on and reception of apostolic Tradition is

an act of communion whereby the Spirit unites the local churches of our day with those that preceded them in the one apostolic faith. The process of tradition entails the constant and perpetual reception and communication of the revealed Word of God in many varied circumstances and continually changing times. The Church's "Amen" to apostolic Tradition is a fruit of the Spirit who constantly guides the disciples into all the truth; that is, into Christ who is the way, the truth and the life (cf. Jn 16.13; 14.6).

17. Tradition expresses the apostolicity of the Church. What the apostles received and proclaimed is now found in the Tradition of the Church where the Word of God is preached and the sacraments of Christ celebrated in the power of the Holy Spirit. The churches today are committed to receiving the one living apostolic Tradition, to ordering their life according to it, and to transmitting it in such a way that the Christ who comes in glory will find the people of God confessing and living the faith once for all entrusted to the saints (cf. Jude 3).

18. Tradition makes the witness of the apostolic community present in the Church today through its corporate *memory*. Through the proclamation of the Word and the celebration of the sacraments the Holy Spirit opens the hearts of believers and manifests the Risen Lord to them. The Spirit, active in the once for all events of the ministry of Jesus, continues to teach the Church, bringing to remembrance what Christ did and said, making present the fruits of his redemptive work and the foretaste of the kingdom (cf. Jn 2.22; 14.26). The purpose of Tradition is fulfilled when, through the Spirit, the Word is received and lived out in faith and hope. The witness of proclamation, sacraments and life in communion is at one and the same time the content of Tradition and its result. Thus memory bears fruit in the faithful life of believers within the communion of their local church.

The Holy Scriptures: The "Yes" of God and the "Amen" of God's People

19. Within Tradition the Scriptures occupy a unique and normative place and belong to what has been given once for all. As the written witness to God's "Yes" they require the Church constantly to measure its teaching, preaching and action against them. "Since the Scriptures are the uniquely inspired witness to divine revelation, the Church's expression of that revelation must be tested by its consonance with Scripture" (*Authority in the Church: Elucidation*, 2). Through the Scriptures God's revelation is made present and transmitted in the life of the Church. The "Yes" of God is recognised in and through the "Amen" of the Church which receives the authentic revelation of God. By receiving certain texts as true witnesses to divine revelation, the Church identified its Holy Scriptures. It regards this corpus alone as the inspired Word of God written and, as such, uniquely authoritative.

20. The Scriptures bring together diverse streams of Jewish and Christian traditions. These traditions reveal the way God's Word has been received, interpreted and passed on in specific contexts according to the needs, the culture, and the circumstances of the people of God. They contain God's revelation of his salvific design, which was realised in Jesus Christ and experienced in the earliest Christian communities. In these communities God's "Yes" was received in a new way. Within the New Testament we can see how the Scriptures of the First Testament were both received as revelation of the one true God and also reinterpreted and re-received as revelation of his final Word in Christ.

21. All the writers of the New Testament were influenced by the experience of their own local communities. What they transmitted, with their own skill and theological insights, records those elements of the Gospel which the churches of their time and in their various

situations kept in their memory. Paul's teaching about the Body of Christ, for instance, owes much to the problems and divisions of the local church in Corinth. When Paul speaks about "our authority which the Lord gave for building you up and not for destroying you" (2 Cor 10.8), he does so in the context of his turbulent relationship with the church of Corinth. Even in the central affirmations of our faith there is often a clear echo of the concrete and sometimes dramatic situation of a local church or of a group of local churches, to which we are indebted for the faithful transmission of apostolic Tradition. The emphasis in the Johannine literature on the presence of the Lord in the flesh of a human body that could be seen and touched both before and after the resurrection (cf. Jn 20.27; 1 Jn 4.2) is linked to the conflict in the Johannine communities on this issue. It is through the struggle of particular communities at particular times to discern God's Word for them that we have in Scripture an authoritative record of the apostolic Tradition which is to be passed from one generation to another and from one church to another, and to which the faithful say "Amen."

22. The formation of the canon of the Scriptures was an integral part of the process of tradition. The Church's recognition of these Scriptures as canonical, after a long period of critical discernment, was at the same time an act of *obedience* and of authority. It was an act of obedience in that the Church discerned and received God's life-giving "Yes" through the Scriptures, accepting them as the norm of faith. It was an act of *authority* in that the Church, under the guidance of the Holy Spirit, received and handed on these texts, declaring that they were inspired and that others were not to be included in the canon.

23. The meaning of the revealed Gospel of God is fully understood only within the Church. God's revelation has been entrusted to a community. The Church cannot properly be described as an aggregate of individual believers, nor can its faith be considered the sum of the beliefs held by individuals. Believers are together the people

of faith because they are incorporated by baptism into a community which receives the canonical Scriptures as the authentic Word of God; they receive faith within this community. The faith of the community precedes the faith of the individual. So, though one person's journey of faith may begin with individual reading of Scripture, it cannot remain there. Individualistic interpretation of the Scriptures is not attuned to the reading of the text within the life of the Church and is incompatible with the nature of the authority of the revealed Word of God (cf. 2 Pet 1.20–21). Word of God and Church of God cannot be put asunder.

Reception and Re-Reception: The Church's "Amen" to the Word of God

24. Throughout the centuries, the Church receives and acknowledges as a gracious gift from God all that it recognises as a true expression of the Tradition which has been once for all delivered to the apostles. This reception is at one and the same time an act of faithfulness and of freedom. The Church must continue faithful so that the Christ who comes in glory will recognise in the Church the community he founded; it must continue to be free to receive the apostolic Tradition in new ways according to the situations by which it is confronted. The Church has the responsibility to hand on the whole apostolic Tradition, even though there may be parts which it finds hard to integrate in its life and worship. It may be that what was of great significance for an earlier generation will again be important in the future, though its importance is not clear in the present.

25. Within the Church the memory of the people of God may be affected or even distorted by human finitude and sin. Even though promised the assistance of the Holy Spirit, the churches from time to time lose sight of aspects of the apostolic Tradition, failing to discern the full vision of the kingdom of God in the light of which we seek to follow Christ. The churches suffer when some element of ecclesial communion has been forgotten, neglected or abused. Fresh recourse to Tradition in a new situation is the means by which

God's revelation in Christ is recalled. This is assisted by the insights of biblical scholars and theologians and the wisdom of holy persons. Thus, there may be a rediscovery of elements that were neglected and a fresh remembrance of the promises of God, leading to renewal of the Church's "Amen". There may also be a sifting of what has been received because some of the formulations of the Tradition are seen to be inadequate or even misleading in a new context. This whole process may be termed *re-reception*.

Catholicity: The "Amen" of the Whole Church

26. There are two dimensions to communion in the apostolic Tradition: diachronic and synchronic. The process of tradition clearly entails the transmission of the Gospel from one generation to another (diachronic). If the Church is to remain united in the truth, it must also entail the communion of the churches in all places in that one Gospel (synchronic). Both are necessary for the catholicity of the Church. Christ promises that the Holy Spirit will keep the essential and saving truth in the memory of the Church, empowering it for mission (cf. Jn 14.26; 15.26–27). This truth has to be transmitted and received anew by the faithful in all ages and in all places throughout the world, in response to the diversity and complexity of human experience. There is no part of humanity, no race, no social condition, no generation, for whom this salvation, communicated in the handing on of the Word of God, is not intended (cf. *Church as Communion*, 34).

27. In the rich diversity of human life, encounter with the living Tradition produces a variety of expressions of the Gospel. Where diverse expressions are faithful to the Word revealed in Jesus Christ and transmitted by the apostolic community, the churches in which they are found are truly in communion. Indeed, this diversity of traditions is the practical manifestation of catholicity and confirms rather than contradicts the vigour of Tradition. As God has created diversity among humans, so the Church's fidelity and identity require not uniformity of expression and formulation at all levels in

all situations, but rather catholic diversity within the unity of communion. This richness of traditions is a vital resource for a reconciled humanity. "Human beings were created by God in his love with such diversity in order that they might participate in that love by sharing with one another both what they have and what they are, thus enriching each other in their mutual communion" (*Church as Communion*, 35).

28. The people of God as a whole is the bearer of the living Tradition. In changing situations producing fresh challenges to the Gospel, the discernment, actualisation and communication of the Word of God is the responsibility of the whole people of God. The Holy Spirit works through all members of the community, using the gifts he gives to each for the good of all. Theologians in particular serve the communion of the whole Church by exploring whether and how new insights should be integrated into the ongoing stream of Tradition. In each community there is an exchange, a mutual give-and-take, in which bishops, clergy and lay people receive from as well as give to others within the whole body.

29. In every Christian who is seeking to be faithful to Christ and is fully incorporated into the life of the Church, there is a *sensus fidei*. This *sensus fidei* may be described as an active capacity for spiritual discernment, an intuition that is formed by worshipping and living in communion as a faithful member of the Church. When this capacity is exercised in concert by the body of the faithful we may speak of the exercise of the *sensus fidelium* (cf. *Authority in the Church: Elucidation*, 3–4). The exercise of the *sensus fidei* by each member of the Church contributes to the formation of the *sensus fidelium* through which the Church as a whole remains faithful to Christ. By the *sensus fidelium*, the whole body contributes to, receives from and treasures the ministry of those within the community who exercise *episcope*, watching over the living memory of the Church (cf. *Authority in the Church I*, 5–6). In diverse ways the "Amen" of the individual believer is thus incorporated within the "Amen" of the whole Church.

30. Those who exercise *episcope* in the Body of Christ must not be separated from the "symphony" of the whole people of God in which they have their part to play. They need to be alert to the *sensus fidelium*, in which they share, if they are to be made aware when something is needed for the well-being and mission of the community, or when some element of the Tradition needs to be received in a fresh way. The charism and function of *episcope* are specifically connected to the *ministry of memory*, which constantly renews the Church in hope. Through such ministry the Holy Spirit keeps alive in the Church the memory of what God did and revealed, and the hope of what God will do to bring all things into unity in Christ. In this way, not only from generation to generation, but also from place to place, the one faith is communicated and lived out. This is the ministry exercised by the bishop, and by ordained persons under the bishop's care, as they proclaim the Word, minister the sacraments, and take their part in administering discipline for the common good. The bishops, the clergy and the other faithful must all recognise and receive what is mediated from God through each other. Thus the *sensus fidelium* of the people of God and the ministry of memory exist together in reciprocal relationship.

31. Anglicans and Roman Catholics can agree in principle on all of the above, but need to make a deliberate effort to retrieve this shared understanding. When Christian communities are in real but imperfect communion they are called to recognise in each other elements of the apostolic Tradition which they may have rejected, forgotten or not yet fully understood. Consequently, they have to receive or reappropriate these elements, and reconsider the ways in which they have separately interpreted the Scriptures. Their life in Christ is enriched when they give to, and receive from, each other. They grow in understanding and experience of their catholicity as the *sensus fidelium* and the ministry of memory interact in the communion of believers. In this economy of giving and receiving within real but imperfect communion, they move closer to an undivided sharing in Christ's one "Amen" to the glory of God.

III. THE EXERCISE OF AUTHORITY IN THE CHURCH

Proclaiming the Gospel: The Exercise of Authority for Mission and Unity

32. The authority which Jesus bestowed on his disciples was, above all, the authority for mission, to preach and to heal (cf. Lk 9.1–2, 10.1). The Risen Christ empowered them to spread the Gospel to the whole world (cf. Mt 28.18–20). In the early Church, the preaching of the Word of God in the power of the Spirit was seen as the defining characteristic of apostolic authority (cf. 1 Cor 1.17, 2.4–5). In the proclamation of Christ crucified, the "Yes" of God to humanity is made a present reality and all are invited to respond with their "Amen." Thus, the exercise of ministerial authority within the Church, not least by those entrusted with the ministry of *episcope*, has a radically missionary dimension. Authority is exercised within the Church for the sake of those outside it, that the Gospel may be proclaimed "in power and in the Holy Spirit and with full conviction" (1 Thess 1.5). This authority enables the whole Church to embody the Gospel and become the missionary and prophetic servant of the Lord.

33. Jesus prayed to the Father that his followers might be one "so that the world may know that you have sent me and have loved them even as you have loved me" (Jn 17.23). When Christians do not agree about the Gospel itself, the preaching of it in power is impaired. When they are not one in faith they cannot be one in life, and so cannot demonstrate fully that they are faithful to the will of God, which is the reconciliation through Christ of all things to the Father (cf. Col 1.20). As long as the Church does not live as the

community of reconciliation God calls it to be, it cannot adequately preach this Gospel or credibly proclaim God's plan to gather his scattered people into unity under Christ as Lord and Saviour (cf. Jn 11.52). Only when all believers are united in the common celebration of the Eucharist (cf. *Church as Communion*, 24) will the God whose purpose it is to bring all things into unity in Christ (cf. Eph 1.10) be truly glorified by the people of God. The challenge and responsibility for those with authority within the Church is so to exercise their ministry that they promote the unity of the whole Church in faith and life in a way that enriches rather than diminishes the legitimate diversity of local churches.

Synodality: The Exercise of Authority in Communion

34. In each local church all the faithful are called to walk together in Christ. The term *synodality* (derived from *syn-hodos* meaning "common way") indicates the manner in which believers and churches are held together in communion as they do this. It expresses their vocation as people of the Way (cf. Acts 9.2) to live, work and journey together in Christ who is the Way (cf. Jn 14.6). They, like their predecessors, follow Jesus on the way (cf. Mk 10.52) until he comes again.

35. Within the communion of local churches the Spirit is at work to shape each church through the grace of reconciliation and communion in Christ. It is only through the activity of the Spirit that the local church can be faithful to the "Amen" of Christ and can be sent into the world to draw all people to participate in this "Amen." Through this presence of the Spirit the local church is maintained in the Tradition. It receives and shares the fullness of the apostolic faith and the means of grace. The Spirit confirms the local church in the truth in such a way that its life embodies the saving truth revealed in Christ. From generation to generation the authority of the living Word should be made present in the local church through all aspects of its life in the world. The way in which authority is

exercised in the structures and corporate life of the Church must be conformed to the mind of Christ (cf. Phil 2.5).

36. The Spirit of Christ endows each bishop with the pastoral authority needed for the effective exercise of *episcope* within a local church. This authority necessarily includes responsibility for making and implementing the decisions that are required to fulfil the office of a bishop for the sake of *koinonia*. Its binding nature is implicit in the bishop's task of teaching the faith through the proclamation and explanation of the Word of God, of providing for the celebration of the sacraments, and of maintaining the Church in holiness and truth. Decisions taken by the bishop in performing this task have an authority which the faithful have a duty to receive and accept (cf. *Authority in the Church II*, 17). By their *sensus fidei* the faithful are able in conscience both to recognise God at work in the bishop's exercise of authority, and also to respond to it as believers. This is what motivates their obedience, an obedience of freedom and not slavery. The jurisdiction of bishops is one consequence of the call they have received to lead their churches in an authentic "Amen"; it is not arbitrary power given to one person over the freedom of others. Within the working of the *sensus fidelium* there is a complementary relationship between the bishop and the rest of the community. In the local church the Eucharist is the fundamental expression of the walking together (synodality) of the people of God. In prayerful dialogue, the president leads the people to make their "Amen" to the eucharistic prayer. In unity of faith with their local bishop, their "Amen" is a living memorial of the Lord's great "Amen" to the will of the Father.

37. The mutual interdependence of all the churches is integral to the reality of the Church as God wills it to be. No local church that participates in the living Tradition can regard itself as self-sufficient. Forms of synodality, then, are needed to manifest the communion of the local churches and to sustain each of them in fidelity to the

Gospel. The ministry of the bishop is crucial, for this ministry serves communion within and among local churches. Their communion with each other is expressed through the incorporation of each bishop into a college of bishops. Bishops are, both personally and collegially, at the service of communion and are concerned for synodality in all its expressions. These expressions have included a wide variety of organs, instruments and institutions, notably synods or councils, local, provincial, worldwide, ecumenical. The maintenance of communion requires that at every level there is a capacity to take decisions appropriate to that level. When those decisions raise serious questions for the wider communion of churches, synodality must find a wider expression.

38. In both our communions, the bishops meet together collegially, not as individuals but as those who have authority within and for the synodal life of the local churches. Consulting the faithful is an aspect of episcopal oversight. Each bishop is both a voice for the local church and one through whom the local church learns from other churches. When bishops take counsel together they seek both to discern and to articulate the *sensus fidelium* as it is present in the local church and in the wider communion of churches. Their role is magisterial: that is, in this communion of the churches, they are to determine what is to be taught as faithful to the apostolic Tradition. Roman Catholics and Anglicans share this understanding of synodality, but express it in different ways.

39. In the Church of England at the time of the English Reformation the tradition of synodality was expressed through the use both of synods (of bishops and clergy) and of Parliament (including bishops and lay people) for the settlement of liturgy, doctrine and church order. The authority of General Councils was also recognised. In the Anglican Communion, new forms of synods came into being during the nineteenth century and the role of the laity in decision making has increased since that time. Although bishops, clergy,

and lay persons consult with each other and legislate together, the responsibility of the bishops remains distinct and crucial. In every part of the Anglican Communion, the bishops bear a unique responsibility of oversight. For example, a diocesan synod can be called only by the bishop, and its decisions can stand only with the bishop's consent. At provincial or national levels, Houses of Bishops exercise a distinctive and unique ministry in relation to matters of doctrine, worship and moral life. Further, though Anglican synods largely use parliamentary procedures, their nature is eucharistic. This is why the bishop as president of the Eucharist appropriately presides at the diocesan synod, which assembles to bring God's redemptive work into the present through the life and activity of the local church. Furthermore, each bishop has not only the *episcope* of the local church but participates in the care of all the churches. This is exercised within each province of the Anglican Communion with the help of organs such as Houses of Bishops and the Provincial and General Synods. In the Anglican Communion as a whole the Primates' Meeting, the Anglican Consultative Council, the Lambeth Conference and the Archbishop of Canterbury serve as instruments of synodality.

40. In the Roman Catholic Church the tradition of synodality has not ceased. After the Reformation, synods of bishops and clergy continued to be held from time to time in different dioceses and regions, and on the universal level three Councils have been held. By the turn of the twentieth century specific meetings of bishops and Episcopal Conferences emerged as means of consultation to enable local churches of a given region to face together the demands of their mission and to deal with new pastoral situations. Since the Second Vatican Council these have become a regular structure in nations and regions. In a decision which received the support of the bishops at that Council, Pope Paul VI instituted the Synod of Bishops to deal with issues concerning the Church's mission throughout the world. The ancient custom of *ad limina* visits to the tombs of the apostles Peter and Paul and to the Bishop of Rome has been

renewed by their visiting not singly but in regional groups. The more recent custom of visits by the Bishop of Rome to local churches has attempted to foster a deeper sense of their belonging to the communion of churches, and to help them be more aware of the situation of others. All these synodal institutions provide the possibility of a growing awareness by both local bishops and the Bishop of Rome of ways of working together in a stronger communion. Complementing this collegial synodality, a growth in synodality at the local level is promoting the active participation of lay persons in the life and mission of the local church.

Perseverance in the Truth: The Exercise of Authority in Teaching

41. In every age Christians have said "Amen" to Christ's promise that the Spirit will guide his Church into all truth. The New Testament frequently echoes this promise by referring to the boldness, assurance and certainty to which Christians can lay claim (cf. Lk 1.4; 1 Thess 2.2; Eph 3.2; Heb 11.1). In their concern to make the Gospel accessible to all who are open to receive it, those charged with the ministry of memory and teaching have accepted new and hitherto unfamiliar expressions of faith. Some of these formulations have initially generated doubt and disagreement about their fidelity to the apostolic Tradition. In the process of testing such formulations, the Church has moved cautiously, but with confidence in the promise of Christ that it will persevere and be maintained in the truth (cf. Mt 16.18; Jn 16.13). This is what is meant by the *indefectibility* of the Church (cf. *Authority in the Church I*, 18; *Authority in the Church II*, 23).

42. In its continuing life, the Church seeks and receives the guidance from the Holy Spirit that keeps its teaching faithful to apostolic Tradition. Within the whole body, the college of bishops is to exercise the ministry of memory to this end. They are to discern and give teaching which may be trusted because it expresses the truth of God surely. In some situations, there will be an urgent need to test new formulations of faith. In specific circumstances, those

with this ministry of oversight (*episcope*), assisted by the Holy Spirit, may together come to a judgement which, being faithful to Scripture and consistent with apostolic Tradition, is preserved from error. By such a judgement, which is a renewed expression of God's one "Yes" in Jesus Christ, the Church is maintained in the truth so that it may continue to offer its "Amen" to the glory of God. This is what is meant when it is affirmed that the Church may teach *infallibly* (see *Authority in the Church II*, 24–28, 32). Such infallible teaching is at the service of the Church's indefectibility.

43. The exercise of teaching authority in the Church, especially in situations of challenge, requires the participation, in their distinctive ways, of the whole body of believers, not only those charged with the ministry of memory. In this participation the *sensus fidelium* is at work. Since it is the faithfulness of the whole people of God that is at stake, reception of teaching is integral to the process. Doctrinal definitions are received as authoritative in virtue of the divine truth they proclaim as well as because of the specific office of the person or persons who proclaim them within the *sensus fidei* of the whole people of God. When the people of God respond by faith and say "Amen" to authoritative teaching it is because they recognise that this teaching expresses the apostolic faith and operates within the authority and truth of Christ, the Head of the Church.[2] The truth and authority of its Head is the source of infallible teaching in the Body of Christ. God's "Yes" revealed in Christ is the standard by which such authoritative teaching is judged. Such teaching is to be welcomed by the people of God as a gift of the Holy Spirit to maintain the Church in the truth of Christ, our "Amen" to God.

---

[2] This has been stated by the Second Vatican Council: "The whole body of the faithful who have an anointing that comes from the holy one (cf. 1 Jn 2.20, 2.27) cannot err in matters of belief. This characteristic is shown in the supernatural appreciation of the faith (*sensus fidei*) of the whole people, when, 'from the bishops to the last of the faithful' they manifest a universal consent in matters of faith and morals" (Dogmatic Constitution on the Church, *Lumen Gentium*, 12).

44. The duty of maintaining the Church in the truth is one of the essential functions of the episcopal college. It has the power to exercise this ministry because it is bound in succession to the apostles, who were the body authorised and sent by Christ to preach the Gospel to all the nations. The authenticity of the teaching of individual bishops is evident when this teaching is in solidarity with that of the whole episcopal college. The exercise of this teaching authority requires that what it teaches be faithful to Holy Scripture and consistent with apostolic Tradition. This is expressed by the teaching of the Second Vatican Council, "This teaching office is not above the Word of God, but serves it" (Dogmatic Constitution on Divine Revelation, *Dei Verbum*, 10).

Primacy: The Exercise of Authority in Collegiality and Conciliarity

45. In the course of history the synodality of the Church has been served through conciliar, collegial and primatial authority. Forms of primacy exist in both the Anglican Communion and in the churches in communion with the Bishop of Rome. Among the latter, the offices of Metropolitan Archbishop or Patriarch of an Eastern Catholic Church are primatial in nature. Each Anglican Province has its Primate and the Primates' Meeting serves the whole Communion. The Archbishop of Canterbury exercises a primatial ministry in the whole Anglican Communion.

46. ARCIC has already recognised that the "pattern of complementary primatial and conciliar aspects of *episcope* serving the *koinonia* of the churches needs to be realised at the universal level" (*Authority in the Church I*, 23). The exigencies of church life call for a specific exercise of *episcope* at the service of the whole Church. In the pattern found in the New Testament one of the twelve is chosen by Jesus Christ to strengthen the others so that they will remain faithful to their mission and in harmony with each other (see the discussion of the Petrine texts in *Authority in the Church II*, 2–5). Augustine of

Hippo expressed well the relationship among Peter, the other apostles and the whole Church, when he said:

> After all, it is not just one man that received these keys, but the Church in its unity. So this is the reason for Peter's acknowledged preeminence, that he stood for the Church's universality and unity, when he was told, *To you I am entrusting*, what has in fact been entrusted to all. I mean to show you that it is the Church which has received the keys of the kingdom of heaven. Listen to what the Lord says in another place to all his apostles: *Receive the Holy Spirit; and straight away, whose sins you forgive, they will be forgiven them; whose sins you retain, they will be retained* (Jn 20.22–23). This refers to the keys, about which is said, *whatever you bind on earth shall be bound in heaven* (Mt 16.19). But that was said to Peter ... Peter at that time stood for the universal Church (*Sermon 295, On the Feast of the Martyrdom of the Apostles Peter and Paul*).

ARCIC has also previously explored the transmission of the primatial ministry exercised by the Bishop of Rome (see *Authority in the Church II*, 6–9). Historically, the Bishop of Rome has exercised such a ministry either for the benefit of the whole Church, as when Leo contributed to the Council of Chalcedon, or for the benefit of a local church, as when Gregory the Great supported Augustine of Canterbury's mission and ordering of the English church. This gift has been welcomed and the ministry of these Bishops of Rome continues to be celebrated liturgically by Anglicans as well as Roman Catholics.

47. Within his wider ministry, the Bishop of Rome offers a specific ministry concerning the discernment of truth, as an expression of universal primacy. This particular service has been the source of difficulties and misunderstandings among the churches. Every solemn definition pronounced from the chair of Peter in the church of Peter and Paul may, however, express only the faith of the Church.

Any such definition is pronounced *within* the college of those who exercise *episcope* and not outside that college. Such authoritative teaching is a particular exercise of the calling and responsibility of the body of bishops to teach and affirm the faith. When the faith is articulated in this way, the Bishop of Rome proclaims the faith of the local churches. It is thus the wholly reliable teaching of the whole Church that is operative in the judgement of the universal primate. In solemnly formulating such teaching, the universal primate must discern and declare, with the assured assistance and guidance of the Holy Spirit, in fidelity to Scripture and Tradition, the authentic faith of the whole Church, that is, the faith proclaimed from the beginning. It is this faith, the faith of all the baptised in communion, and this only, that each bishop utters with the body of bishops in council. It is this faith which the Bishop of Rome in certain circumstances has a duty to discern and make explicit. This form of authoritative teaching has no stronger guarantee from the Spirit than have the solemn definitions of ecumenical councils. The reception of the primacy of the Bishop of Rome entails the recognition of this specific ministry of the universal primate. We believe that this is a gift to be received by all the churches.

48. The ministers God gives the Church to sustain her life are marked by fragility:

> Therefore, since it is by God's mercy that we are engaged in this ministry, we do not lose heart ... But we have this treasure in clay jars, so that it may be made clear that this extraordinary power belongs to God and does not come from us (2 Cor 4.1–7).

It is clear that only by the grace of God does the exercise of authority in the communion of the Church bear the marks of Christ's own authority. This authority is exercised by fragile Christians for the sake of other fragile Christians. This is no less true of the ministry of Peter:

"Simon, Simon, listen! Satan has demanded to sift all of you like wheat, but I have prayed for you that your own faith may not fail; and you, when once you have turned back, strengthen your brothers" (Lk 22.31–32; cf. Jn 21.15–19).

Pope John Paul II makes this clear in *Ut Unum Sint:*

I carry out this duty with the profound conviction that I am obeying the Lord, and with a clear sense of my own human frailty. Indeed, if Christ himself gave Peter this special mission in the Church and exhorted him to strengthen his brethren, he also made clear to him his human weakness and his special need of conversion (*Ut Unum Sint*, 4).

Human weakness and sin do not only affect individual ministers: they can distort the human structuring of authority (cf. Mt 23). Therefore, loyal criticism and reforms are sometimes needed, following the example of Paul (cf. Gal 2.11–14). The consciousness of human frailty in the exercise of authority ensures that Christian ministers remain open to criticism and renewal and above all to exercising authority according to the example and mind of Christ.

Discipline: The Exercise of Authority and the Freedom of Conscience

49. The exercise of authority in the Church is to be recognised and accepted as an instrument of the Spirit of God for the healing of humanity. The exercise of authority must always respect conscience, because the divine work of salvation affirms human freedom. In freely accepting the way of salvation offered through baptism, the Christian disciple also freely takes on the discipline of being a member of the Body of Christ. Because the Church of God is recognised as the community where the divine means of salvation are at work,

the demands of discipleship for the well-being of the entire Christian community cannot be refused. There is also a discipline required in the exercise of authority. Those called to such a ministry must themselves submit to the discipline of Christ, observe the requirements of collegiality and the common good, and duly respect the consciences of those they are called to serve.

The Church's "Amen" to God's "Yes" in the Gospel

50. We have come to a shared understanding of authority by seeing it, in faith, as a manifestation of God's "Yes" to his creation, calling forth the "Amen" of his creatures. God is the source of authority, and the proper exercise of authority is always ordered towards the common good and the good of the person. In a broken world, and to a divided Church, God's "Yes" in Jesus Christ brings the reality of reconciliation, the call to discipleship, and a foretaste of humanity's final goal when through the Spirit all in Christ utter their "Amen" to the glory of God. The "Yes" of God, embodied in Christ, is received in the proclamation and Tradition of the Gospel, in the sacramental life of the Church and in the ways that *episcope* is exercised. When the churches, through their exercise of authority, display the healing and reconciling power of the Gospel, then the wider world is offered a vision of what God intends for all creation. The aim of the exercise of authority and of its reception is to enable the Church to say "Amen" to God's "Yes" in the Gospel.

IV. AGREEMENT IN THE EXERCISE OF AUTHORITY: STEPS TOWARDS VISIBLE UNITY

51. We submit to our respective authorities this agreed statement on authority in the Church. We believe that if this statement about the nature of authority and the manner of its exercise is accepted and acted upon, this issue will no longer be a cause for continued breach of communion between our two churches. Accordingly, we set out below some of the features of this agreement, recent significant developments in each of our communions, and some issues which they still have to face. As we move towards full ecclesial communion, we suggest ways in which our existing communion, albeit imperfect, may be made more visible through the exercise of a renewed collegiality among the bishops and a renewed exercise and reception of universal primacy.

Advances in Agreement

52. The Commission is of the view that we have deepened and extended our agreement on:

- how the authority of Christ is present and active in the Church when the proclamation of God's "Yes" calls forth the "Amen" of all believers (paragraphs 7–18);
- the dynamic interdependence of Scripture and apostolic Tradition and the normative place of Scripture within Tradition (paragraphs 19–23);
- the necessity of constant reception of Scripture and Tradition, and of re-reception in particular circumstances (paragraphs 24–26);
- how the exercise of authority is at the service of personal faith within the life of the Church (paragraphs 23, 29, 49);

- the role of the whole people of God, within which, as teachers of the faith, the bishops have a distinctive voice in forming and expressing the mind of the Church (paragraphs 29–30);
- synodality and its implications for the communion of the whole people of God and of all the local churches as together they seek to follow Christ who is the Way (paragraphs 34–40);
- the essential cooperation of the ministry of *episcope* and the *sensus fidei* of the whole Church in the reception of the Word of God (paragraphs 29, 36, 43);
- the possibility, in certain circumstances, of the Church teaching infallibly at the service of the Church's indefectibility (paragraphs 41–44);
- a universal primacy, exercised collegially in the context of synodality, as integral to *episcope* at the service of universal communion; such a primacy having always been associated with the Bishop and See of Rome (paragraphs 46–48);
- how the ministry of the Bishop of Rome assists the ministry of the whole episcopal body in the context of synodality, promoting the communion of the local churches in their life in Christ and the proclamation of the Gospel (paragraphs 46–48);
- how the Bishop of Rome offers a specific ministry concerning the discernment of truth (paragraph 47).

Significant Developments in Both Communions

53. The Lambeth Conference of 1988 recognised a need to reflect on how the Anglican Communion makes authoritative decisions. At the international level, Anglican instruments of synodality have considerable authority to influence and support provinces, yet none of these instruments has power to overrule a provincial decision, even if it threatens the unity of the Communion. Accordingly, the Lambeth Conference of 1998, in the light of *The Virginia Report* of the Inter-Anglican Theological and Doctrinal Commission, resolved to strengthen these instruments in various ways, particularly the role of the Archbishop of Canterbury and of the Primates' Meeting.

The Conference also requested the Primates' Meeting to initiate a study in each province "on whether effective communion, at all levels, does not require appropriate instruments, with due safeguards, not only for legislation, but also for oversight ... as well as on the issue of a universal ministry in the service of Christian unity" (*Resolution III, 8(h)*). Alongside the autonomy of provinces, Anglicans are coming to see that interdependence among local churches and among provinces is also necessary for fostering communion.

54. The Roman Catholic Church, especially since the Second Vatican Council, has been gradually developing synodal structures for sustaining *koinonia* more effectively. The developing role of national and regional Episcopal Conferences and the regular holding of General Assemblies of the Synod of Bishops demonstrate this evolution. There has also been renewal in the exercise of synodality at the local level, although this varies from place to place. Canonical legislation now requires lay men and women, persons in the religious life, deacons and priests to play a part in parochial and diocesan pastoral councils, diocesan synods and a variety of other bodies, whenever these are convened.

55. In the Anglican Communion there is a reaching towards universal structures which promote *koinonia*, and in the Roman Catholic Church a strengthening of local and intermediate structures. In our view these developments reflect a shared and growing awareness that authority in the Church needs to be properly exercised at all levels. Even so there are still issues to be faced by Anglicans and Roman Catholics on important aspects of the exercise of authority in the service of *koinonia*. The Commission poses some questions frankly but in the conviction that we need the support of one another in responding to them. We believe that in the dynamic and fluid situation in which they are posed, seeking to answer them must go together with developing further steps towards a shared exercise of authority.

Issues Facing Anglicans

56. We have seen that instruments for oversight and decision making are necessary at all levels to support communion. With this in view the Anglican Communion is exploring the development of structures of authority among its provinces. Is the Communion also open to the acceptance of instruments of oversight which would allow decisions to be reached that, in certain circumstances, would bind the whole Church? When major new questions arise which, in fidelity to Scripture and Tradition, require a united response, will these structures assist Anglicans to participate in the *sensus fidelium* with all Christians? To what extent does unilateral action by provinces or dioceses in matters concerning the whole Church, even after consultation has taken place, weaken *koinonia*? Anglicans have shown themselves to be willing to tolerate anomalies for the sake of maintaining communion. Yet this has led to the impairment of communion manifesting itself at the Eucharist, in the exercise of *episcope* and in the interchangeability of ministry. What consequences flow from this? Above all, how will Anglicans address the question of universal primacy as it is emerging from their life together and from ecumenical dialogue?

Issues Facing Roman Catholics

57. The Second Vatican Council has reminded Roman Catholics of how the gifts of God are present in all the people of God. It has also taught the collegiality of the episcopate in its communion with the Bishop of Rome, head of the college. However, is there at all levels effective participation of clergy as well as lay people in emerging synodal bodies? Has the teaching of the Second Vatican Council regarding the collegiality of bishops been implemented sufficiently? Do the actions of bishops reflect sufficient awareness of the extent of the authority they receive through ordination for governing the local church? Has enough provision been made to ensure consultation between the Bishop of Rome and the local churches prior to the making of important decisions affecting either a local church or the whole Church? How is the variety of theological opinion taken

into account when such decisions are made? In supporting the Bishop of Rome in his work of promoting communion among the churches, do the structures and procedures of the Roman Curia adequately respect the exercise of *episcope* at other levels? Above all, how will the Roman Catholic Church address the question of universal primacy as it emerges from "the patient and fraternal dialogue" about the exercise of the office of the Bishop of Rome to which John Paul II has invited "church leaders and their theologians"?

Renewed Collegiality: Making Visible our Existing Communion

58. Anglicans and Roman Catholics are already facing these issues but their resolution may well take some time. However, there is no turning back in our journey towards full ecclesial communion. In the light of our agreement the Commission believes our two communions should make more visible the *koinonia* we already have. Theological dialogue must continue at all levels in the churches, but is not of itself sufficient. For the sake of *koinonia* and a united Christian witness to the world, Anglican and Roman Catholic bishops should find ways of cooperating and developing relationships of mutual accountability in their exercise of oversight. At this new stage we have not only to *do* together whatever we can, but also to *be* together all that our existing *koinonia* allows.

59. Such cooperation in the exercise of *episcope* would involve bishops meeting regularly together at regional and local levels and the participation of bishops from one communion in the international meetings of bishops of the other. Serious consideration could also be given to the association of Anglican bishops with Roman Catholic bishops in their *ad limina* visits to Rome. Wherever possible, bishops should take the opportunity of teaching and acting together in matters of faith and morals. They should also witness together in the public sphere on issues affecting the common good. Specific practical aspects of sharing *episcope* will emerge from local initiatives.

Universal Primacy: A Gift to be Shared

60. The Commission's work has resulted in sufficient agreement on universal primacy as a gift to be shared, for us to propose that such a primacy could be offered and received even before our churches are in full communion. Both Roman Catholics and Anglicans look to this ministry being exercised in collegiality and synodality — a ministry of *servus servorum Dei* (Gregory the Great, cited in *Ut Unum Sint*, 88). We envisage a primacy that will even now help to uphold the legitimate diversity of traditions, strengthening and safeguarding them in fidelity to the Gospel. It will encourage the churches in their mission. This sort of primacy will already assist the Church on earth to be the authentic catholic *koinonia* in which unity does not curtail diversity, and diversity does not endanger but enhances unity. It will be an effective sign for all Christians as to how this gift of God builds up that unity for which Christ prayed.

61. Such a universal primate will exercise leadership in the world and also in both communions, addressing them in a prophetic way. He will promote the common good in ways that are not constrained by sectional interests, and offer a continuing and distinctive teaching ministry, particularly in addressing difficult theological and moral issues. A universal primacy of this style will welcome and protect theological enquiry and other forms of the search for truth, so that their results may enrich and strengthen both human wisdom and the Church's faith. Such a universal primacy might gather the churches in various ways for consultation and discussion.

62. An experience of universal primacy of this kind would confirm two particular conclusions we have reached:

- that Anglicans be open to and desire a recovery and re-reception under certain clear conditions of the exercise of universal primacy by the Bishop of Rome;

- that Roman Catholics be open to and desire a re-reception of the exercise of primacy by the Bishop of Rome and the offering of such a ministry to the whole Church of God.

63. When the real yet imperfect communion between us is made more visible, the web of unity which is woven from communion with God and reconciliation with each other is extended and strengthened. Thus the "Amen" which Anglicans and Roman Catholics say to the one Lord comes closer to being an "Amen" said together by the one holy people witnessing to God's salvation and reconciling love in a broken world.

MEMBERS OF THE COMMISSION

Anglican Members

The Rt Revd Mark Santer, Bishop of Birmingham, UK
(*Co-Chairman*)

The Rt Revd John Baycroft, Bishop of Ottawa, Canada

Dr E. Rozanne Elder, Professor of History, University of Western Michigan, USA

The Revd Professor Jaci Maraschin, Professor of Theology, Ecumenical Institute, Sao Paulo, Brazil

The Revd Canon Richard Marsh, Archbishop of Canterbury's Secretary for Ecumenical Affairs, London, UK *(from 1996)*

The Revd Dr John Muddiman, Fellow and Tutor in Theology, Mansfield College, Oxford, UK

The Rt Revd Michael Nazir-Ali, Bishop of Rochester, UK

The Revd Dr Nicholas Sagovsky, Research Fellow, University of Newcastle, UK

Secretary

The Revd Dr Donald Anderson, Director of Ecumenical Relations 7 Studies *(until 1996)*

The Revd Canon David Hamid, Director of Ecumenical Affairs and Relations, Anglican Communion Office, London, UK *(from 1996)*

The Revd Canon Stephen Platten, Archbishop of Canterbury's Secretary for Ecumenical Affairs *(until 1994)*

Roman Catholic Members

The Rt Revd Cormac Murphy-O'Connor, Bishop of Arundel and Brighton, UK *(Co-Chairman)*

Sister Sara Butler MSBT, Assistant Professor of Systematic Theology, University of St Mary of the Lake, Mundelein, Illinois, USA

The Revd Peter Cross, Professor of Systematic Theology, Catholic Theological College, Clayton, Australia

The Revd Dr Adelbert Denaux, Professor, Faculty of Theology, Catholic University, Leuven, Belgium

The Rt Revd Pierre Duprey, Titular Bishop of Thibare, Secretary, Pontifical Council for Promoting Christian Unity, Vatican City

The Most Revd Patrick A. Kelly, Archbishop of Liverpool, UK *(from 1996)*

The Revd Jean M. R. Tillard OP, Professor, Dominican Faculty of Theology, Ottawa, Canada

The Revd Liam Walsh OP, Professor of Dogmatic Theology, University of Fribourg, Switzerland

The Rt Revd Monsignor William Steele, Episcopal Vicar for Mission and Unity, Diocese of Leeds, UK *(1994–1995)*

Secretary

The Revd Timothy Galligan, Staff Member, Pontifical Council for Christian Unity, Vatican City

World Council of Churches Observer

Professor Dr Michael Root, Trinity Lutheran Seminary, Columbus, Ohio, USA *(from 1995)*

The Revd Dr Günther Gässmann, Director, Faith and Order Commission, WCC, Geneva, Switzerland *(until 1994)*